John H. Caldwell

Slavery and Southern Methodism

two sermons preached in the Methodist church in Newman, Georgia

John H. Caldwell

Slavery and Southern Methodism
two sermons preached in the Methodist church in Newman, Georgia

ISBN/EAN: 9783744731232

Printed in Europe, USA, Canada, Australia, Japan

Cover: Foto ©Lupo / pixelio.de

More available books at **www.hansebooks.com**

SLAVERY

AND

SOUTHERN METHODISM:

TWO SERMONS

PREACHED IN THE

𝔐𝔢𝔱𝔥𝔬𝔡𝔦𝔰𝔱 𝔆𝔥𝔲𝔯𝔠𝔥 𝔦𝔫 𝔑𝔢𝔴𝔪𝔞𝔫, 𝔊𝔢𝔬𝔯𝔤𝔦𝔞.

BY THE PASTOR,

REV. JOHN H. CALDWELL, A. M.,

OF THE GEORGIA CONFERENCE.

PRINTED FOR THE AUTHOR.
1865.

PREFACE.

THE first of the following discourses was delivered on Sunday, the 11th of June. The congregation was a very large one. I had proceeded only to the point where I stated my conviction, that if the institution of slavery had been right God would not have suffered it to be overthrown, when some of the people began to leave the church. I had not passed through all my points of exception to the abuses of the system, when many others left. Others, who stood all this very well, became very indignant as I proceeded to describe the domination of the slave power; some left the church, while others remained to express by their looks and half-suppressed murmurs, I might say almost hisses, their decided disapprobation of my course; so before I got through at least a third of the congregation had left, among them some of my best friends and some of the wealthiest and most influential members and supporters of the Church. The sensation exhibited by my audience, so far from intimidating, only seemed to inspire me with new ardor, so I won for myself the unenviable reputation of a comparison with Beecher: "Beecher," it was said, "could not have surpassed it in fury of denunciation." Long before the sermon was concluded, the following charges were circulating in the streets and through the town against me: That I was an abolitionist; that I had declared myself such for five years, but was afraid to own it before; that the presence of Federal bayonets in the town now enabled me to declare it with impunity; that I was a base hypocrite for cloaking such sentiments while I was an avowed friend and defender of the South during the war; that I had now forsaken my friends and country, and had gone over to the enemy, like a detestable traitor; that I was at least inconsistent with all my former professions and acts. In the mean time, the congregation of the Baptist church was dismissed, and some of the people, hearing the above-mentioned representations, came to the Methodist church to hear for themselves the astounding doctrine. They came in time only to hear the latter part of the sermon, which, disconnected from the former part, confirmed them in the opinion that all they heard of what had gone before was true. The commotion that succeeded during the following week surpassed anything that had ever been witnessed in the town. The people were maddened, enraged, and some even made threats of personal violence. A strange frenzy seized the popular mind, and some even attempted to excite the soldiers against me, alleging that I had charged them with stealing more property within the last four years than all the negroes put together had ever before stolen in all their lives! During all this time, however, my own mind was as calm and serene as a summer evening. I felt no anger, no resentment, but, sinking into the depths of these words, "In quietness and in confidence shall be your strength," I went calmly on in the preparation of the second sermon. I knew in whom I had trusted, and that I had been *moved* by an irrepressible *impulse* (some would scoff were I to call it divine influence) to preach the sermons. I merely alluded in the second to some of the misrepresentations of the first discourse. I have taken my answer to them out of the sermon, as interrupting the course of consecutive argument, and now embody my reply to the principal objections in the following calm address to my congregation, and to my friends at a distance, who have heard the above-mentioned misrepresentations.

1. As to the charge of being an abolitionist, I will let the sermons answer that objection. They speak for themselves.

2. The charge of " inconsistency " is based on the expression, "long-pent-up convictions," and my declaration, mentioned once or twice, that I could not

formerly preach on this subject as I can now.   From
my earliest observation of " the great evil of slavery"
I have had "convictions" that there were many,
many things in the institution that were wrong.   The
Church to which I belong, and of which I have been a
minister for nearly twenty-three years, had the same
sort of "convictions," and so declared itself for a
period of seventy-four years.   Our delegates to the
General Conference of 1844, declared in their "Protest" that the "*whole* Church" had such convictions.
Well, why did I not declare them before? I might ask,
why did not the "whole Church," and especially the
ministry, declare them before? The conduct of many
in this community is a good and valid answer, if such
conduct can excuse the ministers of God for remain-
ing silent in the presence of crying sins.   You know
that the *slave power*, that held even Congress subject
to its will, and could lay its restraining hand upon
the Supreme Court of the United States, and, in de-
fiance of legislative enactments of Northern States,
send an officer and bring back the fugitive slave,
would *have silenced their voices forever* had they pre-
sumed to preach against all the abuses of slavery.
Even now that slavery is *dead*, and I ask you to re-
view all the *moral* aspects of the question and if you
see the wrong to repent of it, some of you would
willingly, perhaps gladly, see me hung by the neck until I am dead.   Yet some of you say the sermon ought

to have been preached long ago, it can do no good now.
Although we could not formerly preach as I have
done recently on the abuses of slavery, I did again
and again declare myself against them as far as I
deemed it *safe* or prudent to do so. I spoke against
the wickedness of our laws on this subject five years
ago, at Palmetto camp-meeting in this county; again
in Savannah, in 1861 and 1862; and again in the
Baptist church in this town last fall. All these sermons are written and are now in my possession. *I
was always careful to write down beforehand what I
had to say on this subject.* Did I not in my "Fast-
Day Sermon," preached from this pulpit over a year
ago, a copy of which some of the hearers asked for
publication, published at their own expense, and circulated among you, declare the innocence of the conservative sentiment? Look at the following passages:
"Antislavery sentiments no doubt existed at the
foundation of the Federal government, but they were
comparatively *innocent* and *harmless;* they engender-
ed no discord, sought the subversion of no government, aimed at annulling no man's rights." Again,
in the concluding call to repentance, I said: "*Let
every cruel tyrant who grinds down the flesh and blood
of his slave, refusing to allow him what is 'just and
equal,' but binding burdens grievous to be borne, admit
that* HIS CRIMES ESPECIALLY *may have provoked that indignation and wrath of God which has*

*been poured out on our guilty land.   O ! if God
has smitten this unhappy country it is for our sins,
and he will not be appeased without repentance."*

Why did not a third of the congregation rush out
of the church when I uttered these words and denounce
me as an abolitionist? Have not others in this community had "convictions" that were unutterable?
Some of you complain bitterly that I said we fought
professedly for liberty, and yet it was to perpetuate
the chains of slavery.   The idea, if not the very language, was put into my mouth by a prominent gentleman in town, a slaveholder, but not a member of
the Church.   A very large slaveholder in the country
said to me, not a month ago, that slavery had occasioned the commission of more sin and had sent more
souls to ruin than any other single thing in this country.   That man was not a member of the Church, yet
there are *professed* Christians who openly assert that
my sermons were instigated *by the devil!* I have
heard sentiments expressed by persons of all classes,
all over this country, against the ruinous tendency of
slavery, and some of those very persons have now
turned against me because I have *openly* preached
what they before felt in their own hearts.   I have
stated my points to ministers and others, and none of
them have seen fit to controvert one of my positions.
The fact is, all have their convictions on this subject.   Are they all hypocrites, because they have not

proclaimed their honest convictions from the house-tops?

Brethren and friends, bear with me, but these sermons have acted as strong drink upon your minds; they have intoxicated you with excitement, almost delirium, and some of you have illustrated the aphorism *in vino veritas*, for you have in your frenzy admitted that there was too *much truth* in the sermon. This is a strange concession in view of your conduct. There was too much, far too much truth to suit the *times* and the *people*.

A minister, deeply moved by the condition of his unfortunate countrymen, earnestly desirous of seeing them pursue a line of conduct that will contribute to their safety and happiness, consults one of his *official* brethren as to the propriety of preaching from a certain text and turning attention to a certain channel of thought. It is deemed eminently fitting that he should do so. He goes upon his knees before God in the closet and beseeches him to aid him in an effort to grasp his subject in all its bearings. He enters his study and consults his authorities, arranges and classifies his matter. New light beams upon his soul, and he begins his preparation. Study, analysis, classification, rouse the latent energies of the mind; it is in a glow of fervid heat, thought awakening thought, emotion kindling emotion. Now both intellect and spirit are in communion with the great invisible

1*

Spirit, and clothing thought in appropriate expression he throws them upon his page, *thoughts that breathe in words that burn.* Specific ideas grow out of generic roots, and all the specific and all the radical forms of thought center in a *higher unity,* and this he finds to be one of the grandest truths in the universe, evolved by the light of revelation thrown upon providential teachings in one of the mightiest political, moral, and warlike movements to be met with in human history. His preparation finished, he enters the pulpit with a soul burdened with the awful truths he has to deliver, oblivious for the time of the fact that he has left his hearers far behind him, struggling amid the maze of perplexity and doubt. He has gathered together and concentrated into one focus the rays of truth which were already glimmering in many of their hearts, but all these rays combined are too much to glare suddenly upon them. The very effulgence dazzles but to blind. Hence misconception, exciting surprise, perhaps anger, leads to an oversight of the plainest distinctions made in the sermon, and a misstatement of what was spoken ensues.

There have been several allusions in the sermons and my printed card to my gradually coming to the light, which I will explain more fully. This was not merely a conviction of the evil tendencies of political secession, for of these I spoke and tried to point them out to many of you before the war. You know that

I did not believe in the policy, but thought it a rashness and madness unparalleled. But when secession did take place, you know that I stood by and defended my country while there was a fragment of hope on which to stand. I did not take this ground on the question of slavery, but, in spite of it, contended alone for the abstract right of independence. But when all was lost, our claim utterly denied, our whole country surrendered to the conqueror, I felt that it was the duty of every good citizen, and especially of every Christian, to submit to the United States authorities, and to acquiesce cheerfully in the terms which they offered us. But my convictions of the evils of slavery were of long standing. They were greatly strengthened when our General Conference struck out of the Discipline everything relating to slavery. That act caused me to feel a sadness which was equaled only by that which I felt when the first gun announced to me the secession of Georgia. I felt an ominous foreboding of future ill. I was opposed to that act of expunging, and because I could not be heard here in Georgia to any good effect, I gave vent to my overcharged heart in writing to the Western Christian Advocate, at Cincinnati. My articles were noticed by some of the Southern Advocates, and "A VOICE FROM THE FAR SOUTH," my *nom de plume*, was represented to his Christian brethren in no enviable light. I came to the conclusion to leave the Church, which had now committed itself fully to the proslavery cause, and go to some Conference in the Methodist Episcopal Church ; I preferred the Baltimore. I accordingly wrote to that great and good man, Dr. Abel Stevens, author of the " History of Methodism," with a view to effect the desired transfer. That good man advised me to await the openings of Providence, *just as if he had a prophetic foresight of these times.* I should have gone to Baltimore at the close of my second year in Savannah, if it had not been for the war.

More than two years ago I came to the conclusion that we would never secure our independence unless we modified the whole system of slavery. From that time I became a warm advocate of gradual emancipation, as without something of this kind we could never secure foreign recognition or aid. I argued this policy with many of you, and I never heard one of you object to it. Finally, I came to the full light of all my present convictions, when the issues of war disclosed this incontestable fact, *that, slavery is dead,* and that " light " is this Providential teaching: *God has* destroyed slavery because of the moral evils inherent in the system which we would not remove. This is a truth which the whole civilized world will accept.

In conclusion, let me beseech you, my countrymen, to beware of those who by their obstinacy encourage a spirit among you which can only entail upon you further misfortune. Beware of those who tell you that slavery is *not* dead, that they will have it still. Brethren, slavery *is* dead; it never more will live *in the land of the free and the home of the brave!* Imitate the example of that illustrious chieftain, who, after fighting for his country as long as there was hope, now *asks* for executive pardon. Beware of the spirit and example of those who would persuade you to live under a government of physical force, rather than a reconstructed civil government, based on a surrender of your long-cherished principles. For your own good, for the good of your posterity, accept the situation as it is, and you may live to see a happy day and a happy country.

SERMON FIRST.

PREACHED JUNE 11, 1865.

SUBJECT: ABUSES OF SLAVERY.

———•••———

Masters, give unto your servants that which is just and equal; knowing that ye also have a Master in heaven. Col. iv. 1.

THE very mention of this subject awakens within us unpleasant memories of the past, reminds us of all that is painful in our present situation, and suggests apprehensions of the future. Our minds run back to those peaceful days, when we fancied we were a free people; when sheltered beneath the ægis of that Constitution which our ancestors fought, suffered and toiled to secure for us; when, united in fraternal sympathy with all who were secured by the same blood-bought rights, we were a great constellation of free communities, which, like those of the heavens, revolved around the Federal compact as a common center; when we looked upon our social system as combining all the elements of beauty, strength and prosperity. But what is our present condition? Is there one among us who fails to grasp the import of events which may be justly ranked among the most important in the annals of Christendom? or one whose pride forbids him to contemplate the stern reality that we, with all our pride of chivalry, are a *conquered* people? Can we calmly consider the naked fact that now stares us in the face, that our destiny is no longer in our own keeping; that our future allotments, be they painful or otherwise, are such as should be *granted*, not such as we may choose? As for our future, how many hearts are now throbbing with intense anxiety; how many entertain apprehensions the most gloomy, and view our situation as extremely disheartening, if not desperate! My own heart is in profound sympathy with my suffering countrymen. They are *my* people; their country is *my* country; their God is *my* God; where they live, I wish to live; where they die, I wish to die; where they are buried, there let me be buried also. When they suffer, I suffer with them; when they weep, let me mingle my tears with theirs; when they rejoice, let me also rejoice in their happiness.

With such feelings, then, excuse me if I venture to-day to say some things which you have not been accustomed to hear from the pulpit. My heart is full of this subject; it is bursting to give vent to long pent-up convictions. Facts which stand before us stern as the decrees of fate, impel me to it.

This text presents one of those human relations which necessarily implies another. The relation of master and servant is, strictly speaking, a correlation, for each implies the existence of the other, and neither could exist without the other. To each branch of the correlation there are affixed specific duties and obligations. The master is commanded to give to his servant that which is *just and equal*, and is reminded of his responsibility to his own Master, who is in heaven. The servant is commanded to obey in all things his earthly master, and is also reminded of *his* responsibility to the same great heavenly Master. He is therefore required to obey, not with eye-service, as men-pleasers do, but in singleness of heart, fearing God ; performing service heartily as unto the Lord, and not unto man. Now you see that these relations and the obligations annexed to them are *mutual ;* they stand over the one against the other ; and they are so knit together, that the one must correspond in all respects to the other. The rectitude of the relation itself therefore depends, in the very nature of things, upon the due performance of the corresponding obligation

I invite your attention to

THE RELATION AND OBLIGATION OF A MASTER.

This relation may be viewed now both retrospectively and prospectively ; both as to what it has been among us, and what it must hereafter be ; the first with special reference to the present condition of our country, the second as regards its future welfare.

The relation as it has existed among us was determined by the proprietary right, the right of *property in man*, and constituted that social state which is *technically* called slavery, or involuntary servitude. This differs from the state of servitude in most countries, where the servile relation depends not upon the proprietary right, but is supposed to be fixed by the voluntary choice of the servant himself. The one is called a *slave*, while the other is denominated a *freeman*. While the slave may suffer many *legal* disabilities which cannot be imposed upon the freeman, the latter may, and often does, suffer many discomforts which never fall to the lot of the slave: still the world, by common consent, calls one a slave and the other a freeman.

From what source do we derive that relation which involves the proprietary right, the legal right of property in man? There are many who question the existence of such right of property, but assert that slavery begins in the perpetration of a *wrong*, that it carries the wrong character along with the relation itself, that the wrong is coexistent and coextensive with that relation, and that no legal enactment can ever cause that to be right which was once in itself *wrong*. This idea is fundamental with that class who espouse the side of *abolitionism*. On the other hand there are those who contend that the relation is *right in itself*, that it has its sanction from God, that the institution as it has existed among us, both in *principle* and *practice*, is *jure divino*, that it is a divine institution, and beneficial to society. This is the view adopted by *proslavery* men.

There is an irreconcilable difference between these two opinions. It is not to be wondered that each side, waxing fiercer and more relentless in advocating its principles, should foment those dissensions, influence those passions, and engender those deadly animosities

which have culminated in a war of four years dura-
tion, the most bloody, vindictive and destructive of
modern times, and which has at last terminated in
the *total destruction* of the institution of slavery.

But is there not a middle ground between these
two extremes? There certainly is, and that ground
is this: *the relation of master is established in the
Bible.* Abraham was a master, and held servants
who were born in his house and bought with his
money. The Israelites were masters, and were expressly allowed to buy servants of one another, and
also of the stranger. Some of the early Christians
were masters, and Paul returned a fugitive servant
to his master. These, with many other instances,
show, that the relation itself does not necessarily in-
volve a moral evil, but rather that it was sanctified
and permitted of God. But to this relation there is
annexed a corresponding duty, a *moral obligation.*
The neglect or performance of that obligation deter-
mines the moral character of slavery. The relation
itself is right, because God does not condemn but
expressly allows it. This obligation is designed to
regulate the *whole practice* of slavery. When, therefore, the practice is regulated by this obligation, the
institution is right; when otherwise, it is wrong. It is
the *practice*, therefore, and this only, which gives to the
institution of slavery in this country a moral character.

Now the slaveholder falls into this error: he sup-
poses that the institution is right, both in principle
and practice, because the relation is right. All our
books written in defence of slavery fall into this mis-
chievous error.

On the other hand, the *ultra* abolitionist arraigns the relation itself, and tries it by the practice; and because he finds things in the practice that are wrong, he condemns the relation itself as a moral evil *per se*, as a sin. But we take the ground that if the practice is right, if the obligation is faithfully discharged, the institution is right; if otherwise, it is wrong. Judged by this severe test, I fear our institution as we have held it in practice, is wrong. Is it too late to pass this judgment on it *now*, seeing it has been effectually destroyed? There are many grave reasons why we should even now pause and solemnly contemplate that institution, especially as there are many among us whose minds are in doubt as to its real nature.

Those who have been in the habit of vindicating the whole system of slavery, as held and practiced among us, on the mere ground of the scriptural rectitude of the master's relation, are now in danger of falling into one of two dangerous errors. The first is INFIDELITY. Already some are fallen into it. Not many months ago, a gentleman of high standing and intelligence remarked to me, "If we fail in this war, I shall then believe that slavery is wrong." I told him that I had taken the same ground at the commencement of the war, and only waited its issues to be *fully* convinced of the moral character of the institution. "But," said he, "*if our slavery is wrong, our Bible is also wrong.*" I told him I would draw no such conclusion, but rather that slavery had been wrong in *practice*, and that we had misinterpreted and misapplied the teachings of the Bible.

The other error is to suppose that Divine Providence has had no participation in the war and its results. Others again complain of the *Justice* of God in this matter. " Why," they ask, " if the institution is right, has God suffered it to be overthrown? Why, after we have prayed so often and so earnestly, have we been doomed to so terrible a failure?" Now, in view of this state of the public mind, I come forth to-day to vindicate the word of *Truth*, and to justify the ways of God with men.

I hold that if our practice had been conformed to the law of God, he would not have suffered the institution to be overthrown.

First, Was our institution right in its origin? Was it conformable to *justice* and *equity?*

It originated in the African slave trade. Mark we have nothing to do with any other system of slavery that ever existed on the earth, except the one that has existed among us. The moral sense of the South long since condemned the African slave trade. All attempts on the part of individuals to revive it, either by smuggling or seeking a repeal of the prohibition, were met with the sternest opposition by the moral and religious convictions of our people. This system was wrong, then, in its origin.

But it does not follow, as some contend, that the wrong thus begun, must, under all circumstances, continue. The sin of the wicked importer of a slave does not attach to the innocent inheritor of the offspring of that slave. The master's relation being recognized in the word of God, and then sanctioned by civil law, it thenceforth becomes one of the relations of civil society, and therefore as innocent in itself as any other relation. The present generation of slaveholders are innocent as regards the origin and establishment of the institution of slavery in this country. If they are guilty, it is because of the *malpractice.*

Had the abolitionist from the beginning, and all the way along, forborne to attack the relation, and only struck at what was immoral in the practice; had the slaveholder held the civil right and all the enactments relating thereto in subordination to the higher authority of the law of God, they had both met upon the common ground of a scriptural institution. There had been no contention, no secession, no war, and the negro, gradually elevated by moral and mental improvement, would in time have been fitted for the enjoyment of freedom; and thus the institution, which originated in the darkest crimes that ever blackened the history of our fallen world, would have been overruled by Providence for the greatest good of both masters and slaves. As it is, an overruling Providence has had a gracious design in permitting the African to be brought to this continent, that he might be educated, Christianized, and fitted for a higher sphere of life. This providential design has been in part realized, and might have been more completely, had we performed our whole duty, and having been thus realized, God speaks to us in the thunder tones of a four years' war, saying, " *The negro shall be free !* "

Will any one doubt that this is the decree of Heaven ? Then he must either come to the conclusion that there is no God, or that this world is governed independently of him, that he concerns himself not with the affairs of mortals. But as Christians we can neither deny the existence or providence of God, therefore we should accept the results of the civil war as his decree, and in meek submission own that he is just.

Secondly, Let us now examine our practice, and see whether it is conformed to the requirements of the Bible.

1. We have denied to the slave education and mental improvement. Do we find that practice sanctioned in the Bible? We know that it is not. Some of us have felt this for many years; we have spoken of it cautiously and prudently; we have at different times and in divers ways sought to remedy the evil, and failed. The negro is a man; he has mind, a soul, a moral faculty within him; and if it is right that these should be developed and improved in the free man, why not also in the slave, since they are both alike accountable to the same God? I am sure we cannot justify this practice from the Bible. Is it either just or equitable to use the means we have acquired from the labor of our slaves to educate our children and leave our servants in total ignorance, and keep laws to prohibit them from learning? Our excuse for keeping them in ignorance has been the intermeddling of abolitionists, to prevent the negroes from reading their publications, which we have usually styled "incendiary," which term we have been in the habit of applying to every form of argument, however mild, that was intended to show us what

was *immoral* in our institution. But if another commit a wrong, it does not justify us in committing further wrong. It furnishes no excuse for shutting out the light from and *binding the chains harder* upon our servants, who were themselves innocent. The plea of necessity does not justify an act so cruel and unjust. In this respect our institution, we must admit, has been *wrong*.

2. Our slaves sustain to one another the relations of husbands and wives, of parents and children, of brothers and sisters. In practice we have dissolved these relations, severed these natural ties, and cruelly sundered these bonds of kindred and affection. Was this giving what was just and equal? Can we find a trace of such an institution in the Bible? If not, our institution has been wrong. I have read all the leading standard works written in the South in defence of slavery, and none of them has ever proved to my mind that in this particular our institution had an element of rectitude. This feature of the system, more than any other, held us up as a spectacle of reproach to the Christian nations of the earth. Can we wonder that they united to crush us?

Many of us felt this; we felt it deeply; who has not felt it when he looked upon the heart-rending scenes of a slave mart? The moral sense of many of our people was shocked, but it was silenced by a power which they could not resist. I could have stood in the very shadow of St. Peter's and attacked Romanism, or in the streets of Constantinople and attacked Mohammedanism, with as much personal security as I could have stood here five years ago and talked as I do now. So much for our boasted freedom of speech!

In 1832 Bishop Hedding was in Augusta, Georgia, and witnessed one of those revolting scenes so common in our Southern cities, a slave auction, in which he saw a weeping mother separated forever from her children, two little creatures, who were hanging to her side and sobbing as if their hearts would break. The good man dropped a tear of compassion, and at the same time made a remark about its "making his blood boil." The next day he was waited on by one of the preachers and notified that his remark had occasioned some excitement, and he was admonished to be prudent. Thus the deepest emotions of the human heart may be stirred, but dare not utter themselves in words. Such has been the character of the institution among us. Do we find that feature of it in the Bible?

3. In practice we ignored the existence of one of the great precepts of Christianity, that concerning the marriage covenant. According to our laws and the practical application of them, the Christian precepts concerning marriage, adultery, and divorce, have no sort of reference to the negro. Is this that Scriptural institution which we have defended as existing by *divine right*, as constituting the normal condition of society, as restoring the patriarchal system, as beautifying and adorning the social state, and contributing so much to the prosperity and happiness of mankind? If so, point us to a trace of our practice in the Bible. We have sought in a quiet way (because we could not in any other) to have this

2

feature changed, but failed. Over a year ago, resolutions were offered before the Georgia Annual Conference, by one of its members, bearing upon this subject. The resolutions were laid on the table, and discussion forbidden as inexpedient and untimely. A mighty power had overawed the ministry, and shut them up against the utterance of their profoundest convictions of truth and right.

4. We passed laws to operate more severely upon the slaves than upon ourselves. Was this just and equal? If so, show it in the Bible!

5. In practice we have made a difference between the freeman and the slave in exacting the penalties of law. If a wrong was committed by a slave upon a white man, he was severely punished; but when the white man committed a wrong upon a slave he nearly always escaped punishment. Many instances have come under my own personal knowledge, and doubtless many have under yours. We have laws which required masters to feed, clothe, and work properly; to punish them for cruelty, for maiming or killing a slave; yet these laws have seldom been enforced, and rarely has any penalty been inflicted. Was this just and equal?

6. We have been accustomed to judge the character of our slaves more severely than we judge our own. We have too often regarded and treated them as thieves, and punished them for petty delinquencies, while in many instances our own evil practices have furnished them an example or an excuse for going astray. Formerly, when anything was stolen in any neighborhood the first suspicions fell on the negroes,

and yet during the past four years more property has
been stolen by white men than all the negroes put together had ever before stolen in all their lives. Why
should we have one standard to judge the negroes and
another to judge ourselves by? Is this just or
equal? I have noticed the tendency in many minds
to elevate the standard of morality for negroes and
depress it for themselves. I have noticed some professors of religion, who were by no means remark-
able for consistency of character, or punctual in the
performance of religious duties, who were loud in
their denunciation of trifling derelictions from the path
of duty among negroes, and who boldly asserted that
they had no confidence in negro religion, that all their
pretensions to piety were hypocritical and deceitful.
Such persons are more apt to pronounce their judgment
upon negro piety than any other class. The best
Christians I have ever known have had the most confidence in the piety of our colored Christians, and the
sorriest professors I have ever known, those less scru-
pulous than others as regards their relative obligations,
have been the most censorious upon the moral and
religious character of the negroes, and have done the
least for their spiritual improvement. There have
ever been a large number of slaveholders in this
class. I never knew many of them to do much
for the establishment of negro missions, but have frequently found them opposed to all such enterprises.
Some of them have been bold enough to declare their
belief that a negro has no soul, that he was made for
no other purpose but to work for a white man, just as
a horse or a mule. They settle large plantations in

the lower part of the state, and in the great river valleys, and stock them with negroes just as they did with mules and cattle. They give themselves no more concern about the moral and intellectual improvement of their slaves than about educating a horse and teaching him the principles of religion. They enter into a nice calculation of how many mules and negroes it will take on a given number of acres to produce a given number of bales of cotton ; how many dollars that cotton will sell for, and what amount must be deducted from the sum for the loss of *a given number of slaves, who must fall victims to the malignant fevers of the locality !* Thus they count their gains at the expense of human suffering and human life ! The life of a negro belonging to such a man is one long, dark night of toil, unillumined by a single ray of hope ! I solemnly declare that I have seen many such masters, and many such slaves.

Is it not astonishing that we have suffered such outrages against humanity to exist so long among us ? Is it any wonder that the curse of God has blasted an institution which has been so greatly abused, and at one dread stroke destroyed it forever ? Look at that curse which Heaven has sent upon us for abusing and perverting an institution which a wise and wholesome legislation might have brought in harmony with .the law of God, but which an unjust and inequitable legislation has abused until it retains not an element of rectitude according to the word of God. Look at that curse, I say ; behold it in ruined commerce and blighted farms, in the smouldering ruins of cities and the desolation of once smiling and fertile plains, in the prostration of every industrial energy and the collapse of every material interest, in the gaunt famine that stalks through the land, and the poverty and ruin that have come upon us. If Babylon and Nineveh and Carthage, if Tyre and Sidon and Jerusalem, were cursed of God, so surely has our own unfortunate country been visited by the stroke of his vengeance, and all *because we would not give that which was just and equal unto our servants.*

How strangely inconsistent have we been! We fought professedly for liberty; and yet it was to perpetuate the chains of slavery. We professed the principles of our revolutionary fathers, and vainly appealed to them as a precedent for our own independence; yet their very first maxim condemned our practice. We professed to hate monarchy and detest tyranny; yet we boasted a KING to whose potent sway all kings and potentates of the earth should bow! Is it any wonder that, attempting to reverse principles so grand, ours should be reversed upon our own heads? That if we, the *free*, invoked the genius of liberty to *forge chains wherewith to bind others*, that very genius should in turn release the captive only to bind his manacles upon our own limbs?

How proud and self-sufficient have we been! We boasted our *might*, our *prowess*, our *talent*. We could circumvent in *diplomacy*, defeat regardless of *numerical strength*, and affected to despise our foes! Is it any wonder that we have been reduced to the necessity of bowing the knee to the power that has subdued us, and begging for a small *favor* as a mere gratuity? The naked alternative is now presented to

every man to stoop or go into poverty or exile. He
that is too stiff to bow now has nothing before him
but the life of a pauper. Is it any wonder that in
the mighty conflict of antagonistic principles, pride,
haughtiness and self-sufficiency should be cast down
into the very dust, and that from this humble attitude
we should be compelled to look up to the rock from
whence we were hewn, even that great rock, the
Federal Union, and *beg* to be lifted up again; and
to that greater Rock on high, and pray to have
our consciences purged from the stains of injustice and
fraud and violence and oppression? Is it any wonder
that we who have grown rich from the toil of those
whom we have ground down by a life of hardship,
granting but a poor return of coarse fare and scanty
raiment, should in return be made *so poor that none
can be found to do us reverence?*

How ignorant, infatuated and stupid have we
been! We shut out the light of knowledge from the
mind of our servant and placed a drawn sword at the
door of his mind, forbidding any wholesome truth to
enter there. We would not ourselves come to the
light that our deeds might be made manifest. We
shut our ears against the remonstrances of the civilized world, and to all their appeals to conscience, to
charity, to justice, to equity, bade them in effect go
about their own business. Is it any wonder that in our
blindness we stumbled on, till now our chosen leaders
are either seeking their safety in flight, or are bound
in chains, while no voice of compassion, no word of
sympathy, comes to us from the civilized world?

How self-righteous have we been! We in effect

said to others, " Stand ye there! We are holier than ye!" We fasted and prayed, yet justified ourselves before God. We reproached our enemies for fighting against the God of heaven, and we defended our institution as one existing by Divine right. We made long prayers, preached war sermons, counted omens by the score which bespoke our ultimate success, and thus we hastened blindly to our ruin. Instead of repenting before high heaven that we had done a great wrong to our fellow man; instead of rectifying that wrong, we refused to amend our laws and do justice and equity. Is it any wonder that we should be stripped of our charge, and that God should say to us now, " Give account of thy stewardship, for thou mayest be no longer steward?"

But why have we shut out the light from our eyes and walked so long in darkness? Why have we so long refused to do justice and equity, and been permitted to hear no voice of warning in our midst against a monstrous iniquity which has shocked the moral sense of the world? I am aware that these are words which once came on the wings of the wind from other climes; but they waked no echo here. We made light of them, and pointed in triumph to the Bible as justifying slavery, and to the institution as of Divine right in spite of its abuses. But the question returns, why? It was because of a power so strong, so great, so determined in its purpose, that it required two millions of armed men to crush it. That power consisted of about *four hundred thousand persons*. They were scattered over a vast territory, yet were as compact as an army of veterans. They

were not armed with bristling bayonets, but with all
the power that wealth, talent, social influence and
political organization could combine. They stood in
their principles and measures from Maryland and
Missouri to the Rio Grande, shoulder to shoulder, knit
together as with the sinews of leviathan. They dif-
fered essentially in many particulars, but they had
the unity of a single person in the one grand aim that
distinguished them from all other persons, that was
to hold about four millions of human beings in *perpetual slavery*. This was the power, the four hundred thousand slaveholders. This was the slave power, the mightiest power for near a century that existed
on this continent. Let us look at the mighty sway
which it held by the civil power and its political influence during all this time.

1. This was the power that crushed out the antislavery sentiment of the South. For a long time after
the revolutionary war, this sentiment was an active
element in society. I can remember well in my boy-
hood to have heard it uttered frequently here in
Georgia. But this mighty power, through the press
and the schools, and the rival political parties, and
penal legislation, and the terrors of persecution, at last
issued its mandates ; bade men hold their tongues,
and utter no blasphemy against the immaculate purity
of that august power. Two missionaries in the Che-
rokee nation, more than thirty years ago, were incar-
cerated in the Georgia penitentiary for disobeying
this imperious decree. This event is one of the recol-
lections of my childhood.

2. This power crushed out the antislavery sentiment of the Church.

The Methodist Episcopal Church was antislavery in sentiment up to the time the Church was divided. For many years after the separation the rules on the subject of slavery were retained in the discipline of the southern Church. They were not expunged until 1858, only seven years ago. The first rule, the one prohibiting the buying or selling of men, women, and children, with an intention to enslave them, was inserted among the General Rules at the General Conference of 1784, at which the Methodist Episcopal Church was organized. This rule was explained by Bishops Coke and Asbury to apply to the purchase or sale of any slave here in America, or for any purchase but to set the slave at liberty. The same General Conference adopted rules prohibiting all slaveholding in the Church, except where the laws of the state prohibited the emancipation of slaves. The language of the rules was objected to in Virginia and in the states further south, as calculated to embarrass the operations of the ministry in preaching the Gospel to the blacks. They were afterward abandoned and others adopted in their place, still censuring the practice of slaveholding, but allowing the retention of the slaveholder in the church. This was a mere concession to the slave power, not a surrender of the principle. Several modifications were made subsequently, all concessions to the slave power, but never for one moment was the principle abandoned. The Church always asserted in the most direct and positive terms the antislavery doctrine. The abolition party in the

2*

Church, at the General Conferences of 1836 and 1840, made desperate efforts to rend the Church, but the conservative antislavery element triumphed, and preserved its unity till 1844. Then came the crash, the rent, the fatal schism which was hailed in South Carolina as "*the first dissolution of the (political) union.*"

Now mark, the Church was not divided by the *antislavery* sentiment, for it had always been antislavery; it was not divided by *abolitionism*, for the abolitionists had been defeated, and the leading agitators had withdrawn from the Church; it was divided by the *slave power*. It happened in this way: The Church had always forbidden, not by any written rule, but by a tacit understanding known to all the ministry and especially the bishops—*the episcopacy to have any connection with slavery.* The General Conference had always refused to elect a slaveholding bishop, and this was known throughout the Church as the standing and immovable sentiment. But one of the bishops, whom we have always loved, and still love, with the knowledge of this fact *kept distinctly before his mind, voluntarily connected himself with slavery.* This was the cause of the separation, and it caused it because the slave power demanded it, and could be appeased in no other way. From that moment the northern branch receded toward abolitionism, and the southern toward *proslaveryism*, until the one adopted a rule to exclude all slaveholders from the church, and the other expunged from the discipline every rule relating to slavery. Thus was the antislavery sentiment crushed out of the Church.

3. This power brought the moral obligation, imposed by the law of God, into subordination to the legal right, established by the civil law. Hence no marriage rite, no education, no emancipation from bondage, could be allowed to the negro ; hence slave marts and slave auctions, with all the horrors attendant on the separation of families and kindred ; hence all discussion by the press, by the pulpit, in legislative hall or elsewhere, in which the right of the master to oppress his slave might be the topic, was disallowed, and penal statutes were made forbidding it.

Having crushed out the antislavery sentiment from among the people and from the Church, this power subsidized everything within its reach to uphold it. The press, the politicians, the teachers, the ministers of religion, were all but so many tools in its hand. The Church and ministry were secularized, and all preferment in Church or state was confined to those who in one way or another preached the gospel of *proslavery !*

4. This power has ruled with absolute and despotic sway. It held the bodies of four millions of slaves in bondage, and at the same time maintained supremacy over the *minds* and *consciences* and *speech* of eight millions of whites. I used often to wonder why none of our bishops, none of our distinguished divines, ever preached on the moral obligations of masters, while they often explained and enforced those of servants. The reason is plain : they were *overawed* by the slave power. It had uttered its mandates and prescribed the metes and bounds of discussion. It had said, in effect, " Thus far, but no farther

you may go in criticising the conduct of masters. You may speak of the relation; call it a *divine right*, establish it in sermon, essay, and book, to be of God's own appointment, and well pleasing in his sight. You may preach to the slave and tell him his whole duty to his master, that he is to obey in all things, not with eye-service, as menpleasers, but doing the master's will with a good heart, for this is required of him by his Master who is in heaven. But as to the practice of the master, as to *his* moral obligation, touch it lightly. You may say something about 'things that are just and equal,' but they must be understood to mean in some places a half pound of meat per day, a peck of corn per week, a hat, blanket, pair of shoes, and three suits of clothing for a year; in other localities, as in lower Carolina and Georgia, you may mention all these *except the meat*. This must be about the range of your suggestions to masters; go beyond it, and you must be reminded that you are uttering sentiments disloyal to the slave power. As for education and marriage, separation of families and kindred, auction sales and negro marts, negro raisers and negro traders, cruel treatment and hard fare, they are not to be mentioned. These are matters pertaining to the civil law, and, being under that, you must obey the powers that be, for they are ordained of God."

Could the most absolute despotism on earth go beyond this, in chaining down the human mind and conscience and speech? You may go to London, and in Westminster or Hyde Park criticize the behavior of the British sovereign; you may go to St. Petersburgh and speak about the Czar himself, but you could not stand on a foot of southern soil and denounce our practice of slavery as immoral, without personal danger. Yet we say that we *have been fighting for liberty*, that we have free speech and a free press! We have had no such thing. We have been *enslaved ourselves!* Our minds, our speech, our consciences, our press, our pulpit, *all* were in abject dependence upon the slave power. I could to-day, perhaps, with the military power of the Federal government established over me, and twenty thousand bayonets in the state to enforce its authority, openly pronounce that government a tyranny without incurring the danger of personal violence; but I could not, when I stood here, five years ago, have denounced our practice of slavery as tyrannical. I should have been forced to leave the state, if an infuriated mob had permitted me to escape.

Have we not been *enslaved*, my brethren and countrymen? But we are now *free!* The same blow which struck off the manacles from the black man has liberated the mind and conscience of the white man.

See to what extent the domination of four hundred thousand persons may reach. The slave power had asserted its authority over the bodies of four millions of blacks, over the minds and speech and consciences of eight millions of whites, and attempted the bold task of extending its imperial domination over thirty millions of people! It was a controlling power in Congress for eighty years. It haughtily declared that it wielded a power that could make half the thrones in Europe espouse its cause. It first demanded and then repealed the Missouri Compromise. It attempted to cross the line and plant slavery upon the soil of Kansas. It had demanded as a constitutional right to go upon any of the public territory of the nation. It had sent the United States Marshal into the heart of New England to arrest and bring back the fugitive. It demanded, in the Charleston Convention, that the same silence which it had already imposed upon the South should now be imposed upon the North; and failing in this, forgetting that the Federal Constitution was its only security against the concentrated vengeance of Christendom, it madly rushed into that secession policy and that rash scheme of independence and empire which wrought its entire overthrow. Surely it has illustrated the truth of the proverb: being often reproved and hardening its neck, it is suddenly destroyed and that without remedy! God called, but it refused, he stretched forth his hand, but it regarded him not; but set at naught all his counsel and would none of his reproof. Now he laughs at its calamity, and mocks when its fear cometh.

5. This power has impoverished our soil. What made these old red hills, these sterile old fields? *Slavery!* Unmindful of the welfare of generations unborn, instead of improving the lands, and increasing their productive capacity, the slave power wrenched from the soil the last dollar it could yield, *to buy another negro, to open another field, to make more cotton, to buy still another negro!* Now these old fields remain the only monument of its former

greatness, the sad memorial of its greed for gold! Will we wonder if the lands which we have so greatly abused should now be wrested from us, to pay the very cost of subduing that power wherein we trusted ? Of that power we had made an idol. We set it up, not only above the thrones of the kings and princes of this world, but above the very throne of God, to make laws wherewith to bind the consciences of men.

6. This is the power that made the war. Slavery made secession and secession made the war. It sent your husbands, brothers and sons to the battle, and their bones lie bleaching upon a thousand gory fields, from Gettysburgh to the plains of Arizona! But that power is fallen. It fell before the mightiest array of military power that ever shook the earth. All nations sent their quotas of troops, and all the North and part of the South marshalled their mighty hosts. The right arm of its strength was cut off by the emancipation proclamation, and the negro himself grasped the musket and fought for freedom. But so great was this power that it fell at last, more by its own succession of blunders than by the might of its adversary. The war, as a sagacious statesmanship might have foreseen, has proved its ruin ; and by its death you are bereaved, as a desolate widow stripped of her dowry, and your children as orphans crying for a piece of bread ! *Is it not so ?*

This power is *dead*, and from the grave which its own suicidal hand hath dug *it never more can rise*. It fell before the majesty of that awful truth, which it had the sophistry to pronounce a lie : *all men are created equal;* it fell before the grandest power beneath the sun, the majestic power of the Federal Union.

A new power is inaugurated in the South, the power of *Freedom.* Never again will you hear the clank of that chain which binds the human form in slavery. Never more will you see a husband ruthlessly torn from the wife he loves, nor the mother from her weeping children. Never more will you read the statute that forbids your fellow man to study letters and gain knowledge. Never more will you behold the human form upon the auctioneer's stand offered to the highest bidder as if it were a piece of merchandise, while the lynx-eyed speculator looks on and bids, as he mentally calculates his profits in a distant mart. Never more will you see a slave-mart, with locks and bars and cells, frowning, like a very prison, upon the street where freemen tread!

A new era has dawned upon the South, an era of light and knowledge, dispelling the shades of a long night of darkness. New light flows in upon our minds; new ideas are afloat in our midst; a new regime takes the place of the old; and society, upturned in its foundations by war, revolution, social and moral disorder, will settle down at last upon a new basis. Servitude will henceforth be voluntary, and the slaveholder, no longer a master in the former sense, will make his contract and pay the hireling his wages. This will be "just and equal;" and while the relation continues without the *proprietary right,* the same moral obligations will rest upon both

masters and servants. Let us, my brethren and countrymen, discharge that obligation, and, in course of
time, the change may be beneficial alike to master
and servant. Let us learn something from past ex-
perience, and the happy effects of this change will
shortly become visible. The waste places will be re-
paired, ruined cities rebuilt, civil government, commerce, agriculture and trade re-established, and we
shall start out rejuvenated upon a new path of enter-
prise and prosperity. Then let us aim for a brighter
and nobler destiny. Let us divest ourselves of all
the old prejudices and animosities. Let us now shake
hands with our late foes beneath the ample folds of
that victorious flag which symbolizes the grandest
power under the canopy of heaven. Let us not
stand back because they have slain our kindred, lest
they draw back because we have slain theirs. Your
only safety is in fraternal union. You will be shortly called upon to meet in a public assembly to peti-
tion the authorities to re-establish the civil government of the state. Let me advise you all to meet
promptly, and publicly pledge your future loyalty
and devotion to the Union. If any man finds himself
excluded from the provisions of amnesty, and affects
stubbornness now, it will only show that he is bent
upon his own ruin. The naked alternative is presented of begging the favor of being included in those
provisions, or choosing the path to poverty, perhaps
to exile. The favor is offered, provided you ask it.
It is no time to manifest pride, it will do you no
good. You are fallen, and lie helpless as a wilted
leaf at the feet of the only man on earth that can do

you any good. There is but one man that can help you, that man is President Johnson. He extends his hand; take hold of it speedily, the sooner the better. That blow is now impending, (the Tax Act) which, if not suspended, will sweep from your path every hope of the future. Beware lest, by taking counsel of your pride, you provoke that last fatal stroke, and like the power you evoked to carry out your wild dream of independence, you fall to rise no more. As for pride, cast it down; there remains no alternative but humiliation or starvation, and he who counsels otherwise is the greatest enemy of your happiness.

I have thus preached to you, my countrymen and brethren, because I would reconcile you to events that are inevitable; because I would awaken within you a desire to look more seriously into those principles wherein you have been educated, and which, as you see, have produced so much mischief to yourselves and your country; and because I would now have you fairly start in the path that will ensure your exemption from still greater misfortunes.

As I have spoken freely this morning to you who lately sustained the relation of masters, I will speak this afternoon to those who sustained to you the relation of slaves. I shall tell them what they already know, *that they are free*, as a necessary result of the war; *they are free*, but that they must remain in their present state until by a formal legislative act they shall be pronounced legally free. I shall endeavor to show them how they must act in future, so that their freedom may be to them a blessing and not a curse.

I will also give you notice now, that on next Sabbath I will continue this subject, in order to show how the power that has so long enthralled our minds and consciences has affected the Church of God.

SERMON SECOND.

PREACHED JUNE 18, 1865.

SUBJECT: THE SLAVERY CONFLICT AND ITS EFFECT UPON THE CHURCH.

SERMON SECOND.

PREACHED JUNE 18, 1865.

SUBJECT: THE SLAVERY CONFLICT AND ITS EFFECT UPON THE CHURCH.

God is our refuge and strength, a very present help in trouble. Therefore will not we fear, though the earth be removed, and though the mountains be carried into the midst of the sea; though the waters thereof roar and be troubled, though the mountains shake with the swelling thereof. Selah. There is a river, the streams whereof shall make glad the city of God, the holy place of the tabernacles of the Most High. God is in the midst of her; she shall not be moved: God shall help her, and that right early. The heathen raged, the kingdoms were moved; he uttered his voice, the earth melted. The LORD of hosts is with us; the God of Jacob is our refuge. Selah. Come, behold the works of the LORD, what desolations he hath made in the earth. He maketh wars to cease unto the end of the earth; he breaketh the bow, and cutteth the spear in sunder: he burneth the chariot in the fire. Be still, and know that I am God; I will be exalted among the heathen, I will be exalted in the earth. The LORD of hosts is with us; the God of Jacob is our refuge. Selah.—*Psalm* xlvi.

THE bold figures in this psalm were probably suggested to the mind of its author by the wars and popular commotions of the times of Eli, Samuel, Saul, and David. These commotions are compared to the

shock of an earthquake, the swelling of mighty
waters, the mountains trembling to their bases and
leaping into the sea, and the sea itself lashing its
storm-beaten waves against the mountain sides.   The
metaphors are strong and grand, but not more so than
become the awful sublimity of the subject.   The
reality of such terrific scenes could scarcely excite
emotions more dreadful than the tramp of invading
armies, the clangor of deadly weapons, the shouts of
embattled hosts rushing to the conflict, and the
shrieks and groans of war's wretched victims.

From such scenes the Psalmist turns his eye to a
spectacle of such serene beauty and loveliness, that
we cannot wonder at his ascribing so great a change
to God, who was his refuge and strength.

From the lofty elevation of Mount Zion he could
look out and survey "the mountains round about
Jerusalem," and the "city of the great king," seated,
like a queen, upon an opposing eminence, with two
beautiful valleys embracing it in their arms.   Down
each of these smiling vales a gentle brook descended,
till, near the base of "Zion's hill," they united, and
rolled their confluent waters along the enchanting
plain.   Was ever landscape so lovely!   Those gentle
brooks united symbolized that spiritual river whose
gentle flow waters "the city of our God."   How
striking the contrast between the two pictures!   One
is the roaring sea, the moving earth, the trembling
mountains, representing the wars, agitations, and
strifes of the world; the other a beautiful river, fed
by tributary streams, descending through a charming
vale, the picture of serene repose.   This picture is

intended to represent the calm quiet, the holy confidence and joy of the Church of God after and amid scenes of danger and battle and political revolution.

What produced so great a change? The providence of God. The Psalmist invites us to contemplate this great truth: "Come, behold the works of the LORD, what desolations he hath made in the earth. He maketh wars to cease unto the end of the earth; he breaketh the bow, and cutteth the spear in sunder; he burneth the chariot in the fire. Be still, and know that I am God; I will be exalted among the heathen, I will be exalted in the earth. The LORD of hosts is with us; the God of Jacob is our refuge."

In all wars and other commotions the hand of God, though not visible, is the all-directing, all-controlling power. He is in every war, in every campaign, in every battle, in every great political and social change, and directs every movement for the accomplishment of his own grand purposes. If war results in the subjugation of a people, or the annihilation of an institution of society, we must accept such result as Heaven's decree, and although we cannot trace the connection between the divine agency and the mere instruments employed by him, nor approve all the principles and measures of those instruments, yet in the end some good will be apparent, and God's name will be exalted; so his people may feel assured in all their sufferings and sorrows that he is their Refuge and Strength. It is this calm confidence in God, this immovable faith in his providence, that brings about that consciousness of security and repose so happily expressed by the Psalmist:

3

"There is a river, the streams whereof shall make glad the city of God, the holy place of the tabernacles of the Most High. God is in the midst of her; she shall not be moved; God shall help her and that right early." This joyful and happy state of Zion succeeds to those scenes of contention and strife alluded to in the first part of the psalm, and which are represented, in the latter part, as coming to an end by means of victory achieved under the direction and control of divine providence.

The Church of God in this country has been for many years in the midst of commotions and agitations growing out of the nature and practice of a social institution, and I come forth to-day to analyze the *principles* involved in the dispute, to exhibit them in some of the *chief points of their antagonism*, and to show the effect *of the conflict upon the Church of God*.

Before proceeding further, let me state that many years ago I provided myself with books on both sides of the slavery question. These works, including journals of General Conferences, comprise about 4,000 pages of printed matter. I have *read* them, *studied* them, analyzed their arguments *pro* and *con*, and I think am prepared to state, define, expound, and elucidate them.

I am not surprised that persons who have never studied much, nor marked the difference between one class of principles and another, should misapprehend some points in my first sermon, and, in a moment of excitement, misstate them to others. It will be seen, however, from what I have said, that my views are not the result of sudden feeling or impulse, but of study and reflection. Now I wish you to understand at the outset, that, for every fact I state, I can point you to the page and paragraph where it may be seen.

First, let us analyze and define Principles.

They consist of three classes denominated respectively, ABOLITIONISM, PROSLAVERYISM, and ANTI-SLAVERYISM or CONSERVATISM.

1. Abolitionists are divided into two classes, *ultra* and *moderate;* but they have a common principle, and differ only as to their *measures.* Their principle is this: ' *It is sin, a high immorality, for any man, under any circumstances, to sustain the relation of master to a slave; that no human being has, under any circumstances, a right to hold property in another human being.*" The principle, expressed in the fewest words, is, "*All slaveholding is sin.*" This being their principle, they are for the immediate abolition of slavery, regardless of consequences; hence the name "abolitionist," one who *subverts, destroys,* or *annuls.* With them the *relation* of a master to a slave is sin, *sin in itself;* and is it not strange that a people who ought to be familiar with the principles involved in a controversy of such long standing, involving, as it does, the moral character of an institution which they have defended as innocent and right, should characterize as an *abolition sermon,* one in which the master's relation was defended from the word of God?

While abolitionists all agree in principle, they disagree as to their measures. In the Church they go for the immediate exclusion of all slaveholders, saying, they " can neither countenance nor fellowship the slaveholder." As a political party I described them in a " Fast-Day Sermon " which I preached from this pulpit over a year ago. That sermon was printed and circulated among you. I here reaffirm every sentiment concerning abolitionism, and would reaffirm every sentiment of patriotism expressed in it, if I could do so without arraying myself against the powers that be, and committing a crime. The principles of ultra abolitionism culminated in their blackest infamy in the " John Brown raid." I abhor both the principles and the measures.

2. The Proslavery principle is, that slavery is a righteous institution, and, as such, it ought to be perpetuated ; hence the name *proslavery*, for slavery, that is, *for its perpetual continuance as it is.* Proslavery men held that the institution as it has existed among us is of *divine appointment*, and beneficial to society. Therefore they regard all the laws to keep the slave in ignorance, to keep him in perpetual bondage, without the possibility of emancipation, and all such as are designed to hold him as a mere chattel, as *right* and *proper.*

These are the chief antagonistic elements which were at work in American society for many years, and which at last produced a severance of ecclesiastical and political bonds, and led to the crash of arms and to the ruin of our section.

3. Antislaveryism is more difficult to define, because it embraces a great many classes who come between the two extremes. In general, an antislavery

man is one who *declares against* slavery, as the name imports. He may declare himself against slavery because he may, like the abolitionist, believe it to be *a sin in itself ;* but he proposes no measures that are harsh, unjust, or inexpedient for its extirpation. This makes a wide difference between him and the abolitionist. To this class the earliest Methodist preachers in America, with Bishops Coke and Asbury, belonged. Those great and good men made the Methodist Episcopal Church *antislavery* at the *very beginning.*

Other antislavery men approach nearer to the proslavery side. They hold that slavery is not of necessity a moral evil *in itself;* but justify the relation of master from the word of God, just as I have done, and only declare against what is *immoral in the practice.*

Now this class included the main body of the Methodist ministry in the South at the time of separation. Dr. Capers wrote an article which was published in the religious papers about that time, *refuting a charge* made in some of the northern papers, that the *southern Church was proslavery.* The charge was *made repeatedly* for a year or two after the division, and as *often refuted,* and the *title disclaimed.* Well then, if the Church was not *proslavery,* what was it? It was not an abolition Church ; then it must have been *antislavery,* and so it *declared* itself through three successive General Conferences, and only expunged that declaration, with strong opposition, at the fourth. The rules on the subject of slavery remained in the book of Discipline until 1858.

That it may appear conclusively to every mind
that I have not misstated the position of the *whole*
Church at the time of separation, I will quote the
following admission of the southern delegates con-
tained in the "Minority Protest:" "*The whole
Church*, by common consent, united in proper effort
for the mitigation and final removal of the evil of
slavery."

Here the evil of slavery is distinctly admitted by
the southern portion of the Church, and it is likewise
admitted that the long-standing declaration against it
had reference to the ultimate extirpation of that evil,
whatever it was, whether the evil *per se* or the circumstances which pertained to the practice, that
were evil. Thus the great conservative element of
the Church was *antislaveryism*.

Secondly, let us notice the Conflict between these
Elements.

There had been little agitation of the subject of
slavery, either in Church or state, prior to the rise
of ultra-abolitionism. Some contention had existed
in the Church, which led to a verbal alteration of the
General Rule and several modifications of the Section on Slavery, until 1824, since which time there
had been no alteration of the Discipline till some years
after the separation. The Church contented itself by
putting upon the record its disapprobation of slavery,
and providing for its extirpation from among its
official members, wherever the laws of the state
would admit of emancipation and allow the liberated
slave to enjoy freedom. "We declare that we are

as much as ever convinced of the great evil of slavery; therefore no slaveholder shall be eligible to any official station in our Church hereafter, when the laws of the state in which he lives will admit of emancipation and permit the liberated slave to enjoy freedom." The second paragraph of the same section provides, that, "when any travelling preacher becomes an owner of a slave or slaves, by any means, he shall forfeit his ministerial character in our Church unless he execute, if it be practicable, a legal emancipation of such slaves, conformably to the laws of the state in which he lives."

The law does not define what sort of "evil" is meant, but leaves every one to the exercise of his own judgment. The ultra-abolitionist may, if he likes, call it a moral evil *per se ;* a sin; the proslavery man may say, it is only in some of its aspects a social and political evil, not a moral evil at all, but *right in itself*, and therefore a proper institution and beneficial to society; the moderate antislavery or conservative man may say, it is not *necessarily* a moral evil, but such only in some of its *circumstances*, and in so far as it is in any of its circumstances it is so far both a political and social evil.

Resting securely upon this ground, the Church had peace, harmony, and prosperity, for many years. The conservative element held the balance of power between the two extremes of abolitionism and proslaveryism, and, for a period of sixty years, kept them from coming into violent collision.

The first serious conflict of the antagonistic extremes arose contemporaneously with the birth of the

kindred ideas of *ecclesiastical and political secession.*
I wish you to mark how these ideas were joined together in their *birth*, where they originated, and how.

On the first of January, 1831, the first number of
an abolition sheet, known as the " Liberator," was
issued from a press in Boston, and was edited by
Wm. L. Garrison. Mr. Garrison quoted largely from
the British abolitionists, and even exceeded them in
the fierceness of his temper and the bitterness of his
epithets. In the following year some copies of this
paper found their way into Georgia, and produced
great indignation among our slaveholders. As yet
the abolitionists had accomplished but little in New
England, and they might, in the course of time, have
exhausted all their wrath against the institution of
slavery in a very harmless way, had it not been for
one of those blunders which seem by some fatality to
have too often characterized our statesmen and legislative assemblies. Had our politicians of that day
looked into their own hearts and studied their own
passions and their tendencies; had they considered the
nature of men in general, they would have known just
how to deal with Mr. Garrison and his paper: *treat
them with perfect silence.* This had been a thousand
times better than to do as they did. The Governor
of Georgia, in compliance with a resolution of the
legislature, offered a reward of $5,000 for the *apprehen-
sion, trial, and conviction of Garrison under the laws
of Georgia !* Now if, in Georgia, the " Liberator " was
an " inflammatory " publication, the reward offered for
him, he being a citizen of another state, must have
been equally so in Massachusetts. Here, then, the

mighty conflict began. It might have been foreseen that this would be regarded as a direct attack made by the legislature and governor of one state upon the freedom of the press in another, and that ten copies of the " Liberator " would be read, and ten abolition societies formed, where but one of either existed before. Nor was this the most of that affair, for the historian informs us that after this, " Garrison left his original ground, discarded the protection of law, and directed his efforts chiefly to the *dissolution of the Union*, and the *overthrow of the civil and religious organizations of the country.*"

This seems to have been the first conception, in New England, of the idea of a dissolution of the political Union on account of slavery, and it carried along with it as a necessary sequence the idea of ecclesiastical disruption. About the same time, Mr. Calhoun, of South Carolina, conceived his grand scheme of a Southern Republic. You see then that *ultra*-abolitionism and *ultra*-proslaveryism jointly conceived, and in widely different localities, gave birth to the idea of a political *disunion*. But the motives were as widely different as the localities and principles from which they sprung. The one wished to destroy the political Union that he might destroy slavery, the other that he might preserve and perpetuate it. See how diverse principles and agencies may unite in a common idea !

Strange to say, the kindred idea of ecclesiastical secession originated in the same localities, and seems in its very inception to be connected with the same agencies. This is a fact worthy of deep attention.

3*

There never was a time when the Methodist Episcopal Church would have elected a slaveholder to the Episcopal office. *Never!* All its history from the beginning, all its enactments on the subject of slavery, all the sentiments of the great mass of the ministry and membership, were so foreign to such an idea, that it was never even deemed necessary to have a written rule forbidding such a thing. It was a well understood and generally admitted fact that this was the *prevailing sense* of the major portion of the Church. The suggestion of "proscription" and "injustice," based, in certain localities, and by a few individuals here and there throughout the South, on this long-standing and acknowledged custom, was itself most *unjust* and *preposterous;* for out of the nine native American ministers who had been elevated to the episcopal dignity, six of them were from slaveholding states, and not one of them a slaveholder. The historical evidence bearing on the point that it was the settled determination of the Church *never* to have a slaveholding bishop, is complete and full. Well, with this long-established usage before their eyes, the delegates of the South Carolina Conference to the General Conference of 1832, earnestly desired that Dr. Capers might be elected a bishop. But he was a *slaveholder*, and this was an insuperable impediment. *The thing could not be done!* The South Carolina preachers muttered their complaints about proscription and injustice, but Dr. Capers did not participate in their prejudices, for he afterwards declared that he "should doubt the *heart* of any southern man who would be willing to go to the North in the office of a bishop, he owning slaves." But this complaint of the South Carolina preachers grew up in the course of four years to embody the idea of ecclesiastical secession, *unless the old usage were abandoned, and a slaveholder admitted to the office of a bishop.* This idea was urged vehemently by Dr. Smith, of Virginia, in a circular which he published in 1836. The General Conference of 1840 passed, however, and no slaveholder was elected, and no attempt was made to divide the Church. Indeed, the Church had now become so settled in the great conservative sentiment that its most devoted friends began to congratulate themselves at the prospect of a long-continued scene of prosperity and harmony, that the disturbing influences arising from the antagonism of the two extremes of abolitionism and proslaveryism were now hushed for a long time, if not forever. Little did they dream that in four years the storm would burst over their heads from a quarter least expected, and rend forever the long-cherished unity of their beloved Methodism!

The Southern " Advocates," in the latter part of 1843, began again to agitate the subject of having a slaveholding bishop, or, if this should be denied them by the majority, attempting to establish a separate organization for the South. The discussion continued for some months, and then suddenly ceased. From January till May, 1844, the papers maintained a mysterious *silence* on the subject of slaveholding bishops. What could be the matter? Why, Bishop Andrew had married, and become, by his own voluntary choice, connected with slavery! Thus the subject became a test question before the General Conference for the first time in its history. Now they had to deal with it as a fact in connection with the pre-existent sentiment known and admitted as such throughout the connection. Dr. Smith, in his circular, had admitted it; Dr. Capers had admitted it; the very argument of the Southern papers admitted it; all admitted it as the prevailing sense of the Church. And to change that deep-rooted conviction was now the determination of a portion of the Church in the South, or dissolve its connection with the Methodist Episcopal Church. Here the idea of ecclesiastical secession, originating in South Carolina, propped up and rendered clamorous by the dominant slave power, had assumed a formidable and practical aspect.

Now, I think that there was a certain connection between this idea of ecclesiastical separation, or *secession*, (for such it was as an *ultimatum*,) and Mr. Calhoun. I cannot trace it so as to be certain of the fact, but the inference rests upon strong circumstantial grounds. It is known that the three leading statesmen of that day, Clay, Webster, and Calhoun, were consulted as to the effect upon the stability of the Union, which a division of the Methodist Episcopal Church would have. They all agreed that it was a step directly toward a dissolution of the great American Union. Clay and Webster, on this account, deplored any such division, but Calhoun both approved and encouraged it, knowing that it tended directly to the accomplishment of his own scheme. It is certain that Dr. Capers consulted him on this point, and it is equally certain that he lent the sanction of his name and great influence to it. In a letter which he is supposed to have written upon this subject to a distinguished divine of the South Carolina Conference, he connects the idea with political secession, and says: "A dissolution of the Union will throw the South, with Texas affiliated, into a new republic, with Great Britain to guarantee its independence." His reasons for this guarantee of independence by Great Britain were the old "King Cotton" arguments, about which we heard so much for some years before the war. Thus it seems that there are good grounds to infer that the idea of a division of the Church was connected in its very inception with Mr. Calhoun and his idea of political secession. When the Church was divided the event was hailed by the Governor of South Carolina "*as the first dissolution of the Union*," so confident were all the ultra-proslavery politicians that it had this inevitable tendency. So these kindred ideas had a common origin both as to agency and locality in the South.

I will now show you how they had a common origin in another quarter. In 1834, two years after the first murmur against the old usage was uttered in the Church among us, several leading Methodist divines of New England became abolitionists, and agitated the subject in popular assemblies, at camp-meetings, and in annual conferences. They read and extensively circulated the "Liberator." The result was, that a majority of the New England preachers became abolitionists, and their doctrine was made the test in the election of delegates to the General Conference of 1836. They were opposed by Bishops

Hedding and Emory, and Drs. Fisk and Abel Stevens. All the remonstrances of those good men did them no good. They rushed madly on, determined, as they said, to "split the great Methodist prop to slavery," by which they meant the Church. The commotion between those abolition preachers with Garrison and his paper shows the general disorganizing tendency of their views. Thus in New England and in South Carolina these principles and agencies began about the same time with that "irrepressible conflict" which was to terminate in the present condition of slavery.

Now what kept the belligerent extremes so long asunder? It was the old conservative element at the North, with such men as Hedding, Emory, Fisk, Stevens, and others at its head. They, in effect, said to their Southern brethren, "Let us alone, we will fight this battle for you. Nothing that you can say or do will satisfy our misguided brethren, who have been carried off by the ultra-abolition mania. They consider you as sold to the slave power, and the apologists of all its abominations." They did fight that battle, and for doing so were reproached as "pro-slavery men." But the disaffected party was overthrown at the General Conference, and, unable to accomplish their purposes, the principal agitators withdrew from the Church. Thus tranquillity was restored to our Zion.

What brought the antagonistic parties in collision again? That fatal and ever-to-be-lamented act of our venerable and beloved Bishop Andrew, *his voluntary connection with slavery*. Previously to this he had become a slaveholder by bequest and inheritance without his own choice, but no account was taken of this. If the fact was known at the North, as it must have been among some of the conservative brethren, it only shows the *forbearance* of the Church, and its willingness to exculpate the bishop of an intention to infringe in the least the established usage, and does not show any disposition to relinquish the principle, or yield it even to the most urgent demands of the proslavery party. But when his voluntary choice to infringe that principle was made known, when it had become apparent to all that he had *assumed the responsibility* of making it a practical test question in the General Conference, his act became *insufferable*. His defense, which was continued for many days in the General Conference, rested chiefly upon the dubious import of two words in the second paragraph of the section on slavery, the words "traveling preacher." The whole plea was that "traveling preacher" included the bishop as well as the inferior grades of the ministry, and therefore this was the law covering his case, and hence any act of censure was *extra-judicial*. But the whole language of the Discipline, the *usus loquendi* of the whole Church, were against this construction; sufficiently so, at least, to make it extremely doubtful without a precedent authoritative construction, and by no means as authoritatively binding as the antecedent *practice* of the Church. Thirteen annual conferences all at once *assumed* that the section on slavery was a " compromise," a " treaty," a " compact " between the conferences in the slaveholding and the non-slaveholding states, while *twenty* conferences, embracing near two thirds of the Church, held that it

was a mere *concession to the slave power* for the sake
of the peace and welfare of the Church in the South,
for the unrestricted exercise of ministerial functions
among masters and slaves.   And because the minority
had become incensed against the majority for express-
ing their "sense" of the conduct of Bishop Andrew
in the mildest form in which words could express
that judgment, they determined to withdraw and
form a separate organization.   Thus was the Church
divided.

Our people generally do not read history.   They
catch it up from their politicians, newspapers, and
ministers in detached fragments, and can seldom trace
the connection of events.   When they do read it, it is
rarely with a philosophic eye, looking into first principles and causes, tracing events from antecedent to
sequence like the successive links of a chain, through
a long series which terminate in some great paramount fact.   Behold here, my brethren and countrymen, some of those remote causes which stand indis-
solubly connected with all the astounding events of
the past four years.   You have here some of the links
of that hitherto invisible chain of facts which stand
connected with every ruined city and every devastated
section and every broken heart and every mutilated
form in this land of wretchedness and woe!   Brethren,
I have shown you a history that you never knew before.   Your politicians hid it from your view when
they addressed you from the "stump," and only let
you see enough to inflame your hatred toward the
North, and all for their own ambitious purposes.
Your secular press would not show you this history,

because for the most part it was the mere tool of faction ; your religious press could not, because it must advocate only such doctrines and detail such facts as may suit the tastes and contribute to the ends of that power which had enslaved it; your ministers did not tell you this history, because many of them were ignorant of it themselves, and those who knew it *would not tell you.* O that our politicians had been wise and disinterested patriots! O that our Church and party organs had taught the people wisdom, stemming the tide of unpopularity, biding their time for truth to assert and maintain her authority! O that our ministry had taught us like faithful watchmen upon the walls of Zion! Then had not our feet run into forbidden paths, and our war-scarred country would to-day be free and happy, with no signs of ravage and desolation around us! But what, O my heart-stricken countrymen, is the great paramount fact which this long and desperate conflict has disclosed? Is it not this, *we have sinned, and God has smitten us?* O hide not the appalling truth from your view. God has spoken in the thunder-shock of battle and told us that we have sinned. By the triumph of our foes he has cast both the horse and his rider into a dead sleep ; he has broke the bow and cut the spear in sunder ; he has burnt the chariot in the fire, and caused war to cease through all this land. And now he says to us, "Be still, and know that I am God!" He would have us feel and acknowledge that his hand is in our humiliation, that he hath laid our glory in the dust, and all to make us confess that we have sinned. He shows us to-day by the light of his marvelous providence that we have sinned, and by the light of history what our Church and ministry have done to bring all this ruin upon us.

Thirdly, let us mark the effect which this contest has had upon our Church.

The following may be regarded as the principal constituent elements of a prosperous Church :

1. A sound and healthy religious literature.

2. A devoted ministry, preaching the pure Gospel of Christ.

3. A well-instructed and pious membership, *walking in all the commandments and ordinances of the Lord blameless.*

4. The wholesome and salutary education of the young.

By these rules let us try :

1. *Our Literature.*

The Methodist Book Concern of New York grew up from a small insignificant beginning to a great mammoth establishment, worth six or seven hundred thousand dollars. It disseminated a sound, healthy religious literature throughout the whole extent of the connection. It was like a *great funded charity,* distributing its annual profits among all the superannuated ministers, and the widows and the orphans of deceased ministers, in a just and equitable ratio, throughout the entire connection both north and south. Now mark one very significant fact: that Concern had never published and disseminated any ultra-abolition doctrine ; never in a solitary instance that I remember. In this particular the Book Concern had given us *no cause of offence*. Mark again, the religious journals—"Advocates" as they were generally called—had never propagated any such doctrine. On the contrary, they all occupied conservative ground, defended the unity of the Church against the disorganizing tendencies of the conflicting extremes, and contributed all they could to the ultimate overthrow of the abolition radicals. Our literature was free from the taint of abolition *ultraism*, nothing of the kind could find its way into the books and periodicals of the Church.

The lamentable separation occasioned a dispute about a division of the Church property, we demanding in particular an equitable partition of the Book Concern. I do not say it was not right that we should have our just proportion, though in the view of the majority there were constitutional difficulties in the way. The majority could not, by agreeing to the plan of separation, bind their constituents, and the difficulties were not removed. We went before Cæsar to claim our share, and he granted our request, that is, we sued them at the law and recovered our "rights." I do not say it was not right for us to sue and recover our property if we could get it in no other way, for I will not set my judgment against that of the Supreme Court; but in going to law with our brethren we went directly in the face of a Christian precept. We got our portion and then set up for ourselves a publishing house in Nashville. Now mark another significant fact, very significant if we view it in connection with the principles we have argued, and the disastrous results of the late war. *We commenced forthwith to defend pro-slaveryism!* About a year after the publishing house went into operation it issued Dr. W. A. Smith's book on the "Philosophy and Practice of Slavery." In the "Philosophy" he endeavors to prove that slavery—American slavery—is *right in itself*, that it is a divine institution. He says in the very outset, "The position I propose to maintain in these lectures is, that slavery *per se* is right; or the great abstract principle of slavery is right." In the "Practice" he vindicates the policy of the South, the laws on the subject of slavery, on the score of *necessity*, and declares that policy to be both wise and humane. Though the lecture on the "Duties of Masters to Slaves" contains some excellent suggestions, the *evil practices* of slavery are nowhere set forth in a prominent light, but are justified and defended, so far as the "southern policy" embraces inherently those evils.

He admits a pre-existent antislavery sentiment throughout the South, and avows his intention in the "lectures" to eradicate it. In short, the sole purpose of the book is to prop up and defend the principle and practice of proslaveryism. This book must have had a powerful influence over the minds of our ministers, for it was hardly two years from the time it was issued till the General Conference struck out of the book of Discipline its time-honored declaration against slavery. Through sunshine and storm, amid prosperous and adverse scenes, that declaration had stood for a period of seventy-four years as a testimony to the Christian nations of the earth that the great body of Methodist people, even here in the South, stood committed to the gradual mitigation if not final extirpation of the evil of slavery. But now the Methodist publishing house at Nashville stood forth before the world fairly committed as the propagandist of proslavery doctrines. That was the last meeting of the General Conference of the Methodist Episcopal Church, South!

2. Let us try our ministry by the rule laid down: *a devoted ministry, preaching the pure Gospel of Christ.* Have we been thus devoted? Have we practiced on the motto of our great founder, *homo unius libri?* Have we been emphatically men of *one* Book and *one* calling, or have we mixed along with our public ministrations the elements of a false moral and political philosophy, which have detracted from our usefulness and contributed to the present deplorable condition of Church and state? Have we preached the pure Gospel of Christ as respects all the relative and social duties? Who among us has ever lifted up a true, manly, martyr-like remonstrance against the crying evils of slavery? There has not been one martyr to the principles of true conservatism. Our principles and measures have not tended to preserve what was *established*, but have tended directly to the destruction of both Church and state. I accept the light which present events cast upon our past history, connecting it with the present, as the great Providential teaching. I must accept this or exclude divine providence from any share in the events of human history, and then my mind would sink into the fathomless depths of skepticism. Yet there are men among us—if not in the ministry—in the Church and in the world, who hate the very name of conservatism

as implying a base surrender of the very principles of our education. Some of our ministers have actually turned apostles of proslaveryism. Dr. Smith not only spoke the substance of his lectures from his chair of Moral Philosophy to the students of Randolph Macon College, but, as he informs us, "on various popular occasions in Virginia and North Carolina." One minister, I believe, wrote a book expressly to prove that the African race had inherited the curse pronounced against Canaan, the son of Ham, and that that curse was *perpetual slavery!*

3. Let us try the Church by the standard laid down: *a well-instructed and pious membership, walking in all the commandments and ordinances of the Lord blameless.* Have you been properly instructed, my brethren; I mean in respect to this institution of slavery? Have you been taught the real nature involved in the principles of that institution? Were you never able to penetrate the deep motives and design of the men who taught you that the *principle* and *practice* of slavery were alike right and acceptable to God? Did you ever understand how those who would persuade you that there was nothing wrong in this institution could not remove those irrepressible misgivings, those occasional convictions and somber forebodings of ill, which would spring up in your minds in spite of their arguments? Did any one ever faithfully admonish you of those deep-seated inherent evils connected with slavery by all the sanctions of public law? Did you ever understand the motives of those who, to perpetuate such an odious system of laws, would undermine those civil and religious obli-

gations which once bound you in affectionate unity to the same government and the same Church? Have you, as a Christian people, walked in *all* the commandments and ordinances of the Lord? Have you, as giving to your servants the things that are "just and equal," in matters of food and clothing, instruction and pure morals in their marriage relations and their family affections—in all social and relative duties? Have you been *blameless* in all these particulars?

4. Let us apply the rule as regards the instruction of our children: *a wholesome and salutary education.* Where have they had it as respects the "peculiar institution?" It is my solemn conviction, my brethren, that we have all been under the influence of a most fatal system of education in regard to slavery. Our children have grown up under the same influences, and have imbibed those principles which have resulted in a wide-spread and universal ruin to the great and prosperous country we once had. The vail of ignorance is still spread over the eyes of the great mass of our population, and from many of them it will never be removed while they live in this world. Let me show you how this false education has been most successfully imparted. In most of our colleges and High Schools "Wayland's Moral Science" was for a long time the text-book in the department of moral philosophy. His views on the subject of slavery are well known. To counteract their tendency a system of strictures was adopted in nearly every college. This was the purpose of Dr. Smith's lectures. As conservatism had for some years been greatly on

the decline in the South before the war, and as proslaveryism had become the prevailing sentiment both in
Church and state, all our professors in the department
of Moral Philosophy conformed their lectures to this
dominant sentiment. The consequence was that our
children were trained up to cherish the bitterest en-
mity toward the people of the North, and with all
their ideas bent in the direction of an ultimate dissolution of the Union. Hence, as soon as the war broke
out, the boys even of the freshman and sophomore
classes abandoned their studies in many instances, and
volunteered to fight the Yankees. An irrepressible
desire seized upon our youthful population, they threw
down their text-books and grasped the musket. The
schools and colleges were nearly all broken up, and
the cause of education has suffered for four years.

Now, look at the effect of this mighty contest upon
all these elements of prosperity in the Church. Our
publishing house and Advocates, where are they?
Echo answers, *Where!* We called upon Cæsar to
give us our just proportion of the Book Concern; he
did so, *and now comes to claim it for himself under
the act of confiscation.* The last of the Advocates, I
believe, has perished amid those flames of civil war
which the principles and measures they advocated
helped to kindle. Look at our ministry! See you
not the languor, dullness, and insipidity which, ever
since 1858, have marked our discourses? See you
not a marked departure of that demonstration and
power of the Spirit with which we once proclaimed
the Gospel? And what is the state of our Zion? O,
behold the Churches which have been desecrated, de-

molished or forsaken. See the districts, stations, missions, and circuits that have been broken up and abandoned! See the deadness and insensibility among the membership! See all over this unhappy land how barrenness and blight have come upon the Church! Is she not as a deserted village, as a barren wilderness, a blighted vineyard, a parched and sun-smitten desert? And where are our schools and colleges? Not a college in operation throughout all this desolated land! The walls of many of them have crumbled to their foundations, and nearly all bear some marks of the universal ruin! Dilapidation and decay, dissolution, wretchedness, seem stamped upon every interest of Christianity! O, that I had every editor and every minister, every teacher and member and pupil throughout our vast communion before me to-day, that I might portray before them the enormity of the ruin which the principles we have inculcated have brought upon the Church! I speak not now to the few who hear me, but to the Church and to the nation, trusting that ere long the sentiments may be re-echoed by millions of hearts, and that a thousand tongues of fire may proclaim them.

A principle was laid down many years ago, by one of the most illustrious of our southern statesmen, and a declaration based upon it which deserves particular attention. The principle was this, that slavery is an evil, a sin, *per se*. That man was not a believer in the Bible; he was a freethinker, a southern man, a slaveholder, and filled successively the chairs of Vice-President and President of the United States. That man was THOMAS JEFFERSON, the illustrious father of

4

the democratic party, whose opinions in politics have been the standard of southern proslavery democrats. He based his principle not on the Bible, but on his first political maxim, that "all men are created equal," equal as to natural right. He based on this principle the following declaration, which proved prophetic: "There is no attribute in the divine mind which can take sides with the whites in a controversy with the races." That prophecy has been fulfilled. We all thought that God was with us in the beginning of our great struggle. For a long time I thought so myself. In nearly all the great battles we were at first successful, and my fancy dwelt on many, many incidents which I was pleased to note as instances of providential interposition in our favor. But we were all mistaken. When our every hope had failed us, and the whole country was surrendered to the Federal army, my mind at once accepted the only solution of the great providential problem of the war—*God has destroyed slavery because of our sins in connection with it as a system!* I can accept no other solution that would not dishonor God.

Now, I ask—in view of this prophetic declaration of Thomas Jefferson, who at best was but a mere theist according to nature, but who nevertheless believed that the God of nature would take the part of the oppressed—*if we have not sinned?* I ask you in view of the argument presented in these two sermons, *have we not sinned?* Have we not, as the white race of this southern clime, sinned? We the people have sinned because we make our own laws, through our representatives, and they have been *bad laws.* All of us who voted or could influence voters have sinned in that we failed to make any effort to change those bad laws. God has spoken to us in the thunder tones of a thousand battles, and told us that we have sinned. He now speaks to us by the all-surrounding ruin and desolation, and tells us that we have sinned. And now, while we writhe and agonize under the appalling stroke of his righteous indignation, he tells us, " Be still, and know that I am God."

" But then if we have sinned are we not ruined ? " No ! Not if we repent. Here then I reach my final reason for preaching these sermons now. I intimated in the outset that there were many grave reasons for it. The danger of infidelity was one of them, the complaints of some against Providence another, to reconcile you to inevitable fate another, to induce my hearers to exercise a spirit of submission to the Constitution and laws of the Government that has subdued them another, to persuade them to act prudently, so as, if possible, to avert other evils that are impending, and to convince them of the evils inherent in the system of slavery, as held and practiced by us, so they might *conscientiously* do what they are now obliged to, *swear to abolish it forever.* How any honest man, to say nothing of a Christian, can take a solemn oath before Almighty God to abolish an institution which he believes to be of divine right, *and reconcile it to his conscience*, I am unable to conceive. As for myself, if I did not believe that slavery is wrong as we have held and practiced it, *I would go into exile before I would take that oath.* But the gravest reason of all is this : *If we have sinned we must repent.* "He that covereth his sins shall not prosper; but whoso confesseth and forsaketh them shall have mercy." O, let us repent and God will heal our broken hearts. Now that he, by his amazing providence, has brought us to the verge of poverty and ruin, let us repent. If we will but humble ourselves under his mighty hand and repent, what a happy change shall we behold! We shall be a poorer, but a humbler and happier people. It is the broken and contrite heart that God will heal and bless; it is the humble mind in which he will set up his abode. Living to labor and satisfy the wants of nature, not to grow rich and revel in luxury, we shall learn the secret of true happiness, sweet contentment. God will be our light and salvation, and the peace that passeth understanding will take the place of carking care. Angry passions will be hushed up, all murmuring thoughts and vain be dispelled from the mind, and grace, rich grace, will secretly reign in our hearts through righteousness unto eternal life. God's desecrated and forsaken temples will be rebuilt and reopened; thrift and industry will soon reappear, and the land, so long desolated and trodden down, will smile under the hand of skillful tillage, while the schools and colleges, so long shut up, will be crowded again with studious youth. A pure and blessed Gospel will be proclaimed in our midst, the feet of the stricken and afflicted ones shall again walk in the way to Zion's hill, and the weary, heavy-laden, woe-begone spirit find rest in the sanctuary of God. Then shall we realize the picture of the psalm, "There is a river, the streams whereof shall make glad the city of God, the holy place of the

tabernacles of the Most High. God is in the midst
of her; she shall not be moved; God shall help her,
and that right early." Oh, that blessed river of salvation shall flow through our sanctuary again; its
heavenly streams, long obstructed by ignorance and
folly and sin, shall pour their living waters through
our hearts and cleanse all our filth away. Out of our
inmost souls shall flow that living water in the sanctuary, in the Sunday school, in the family circle, and
bring servants and children and neighbors all under
its hallowed influence. Then shall the revival begin
that will extend from heart to heart, from family to
family, from church to church, all over this heaven-
smitten land, and we shall forget the ill fortune of the
present in the dawn of a new day of happiness for us
and our children. And shall these two sermons contribute anything to a result so glorious? If so, I send
them forth on this divine mission. Go, ye little fledg-
lings of my disenthralled heart, and bear the message
of out-spoken truth to my weeping countrymen. Bear
these words that kill and make alive, till every minister and member of the Church, feeling their burning
power, shall rise to a new and holier life. Bear them,
ye winds, to distant climes, and let the world know
that free speech has at last attacked the dragon of
iniquity in the stronghold of its power, even in the
hearts of my own people, where it had long entrench-
ed itself in the very guise of innocence! Go, O ye
seedlings of precious truth, and let the world know
that we, the people of the South, conquer even in our
fall; that we now subdue all human pride and angry
passions, and rise to live and live forever! O, tell

it out to all mankind, that we are a regenerated nation, and henceforth will join the universal Church of the Redeemer in the grand march to the millennial day!

ALMIGHTY and most merciful God, thou art the Father of spirits, and we are thy offspring. Thou rulest over all in heaven above and on the earth beneath. Thy providential care is over all thy creatures, and thou teachest by thy word and providence that thou art watchful over them through all the events of their lives, and art with thy people amid all the afflictions which befall them in this world. May we bow in meek submission at thy feet, and, with our hearts stilled into awful reverence before thy divine majesty, acknowledge that thou alone art God. Help us to praise thee, that thou art exalted in all the earth, and that thou art the refuge and strength of all who put their trust in thee. Thou, O great and mighty Creator, hast made of one blood all nations of men to dwell on all the face of the earth; and though it hath pleased thee to ordain various ranks and conditions of men in society, and to establish various relations among them, appointing some to command and others to obey, yet, O just and holy God, thou hast taught us that with thee there is no respect of persons. Thy law binds us to love all our fellow-men, regardless of their social condition, as ourselves, and to do unto all men as we would have them do unto us. But, O Lord God most holy, we do most truly and humbly confess before thee, that we have sinned against thy most pure and just law of love, in that we have made merchandise of the souls and bodies of our fellow-men; we have made laws which did most cruelly oppress them; we virtually set at naught thy marriage covenant among them, and did too often put asunder those whom thou didst join together; we shut out the light of knowledge from their minds; we have failed too frequently to comply with thy most righteous command to give unto them the things that are just and equal; and we have committed many acts of violence and injury against them.

And now we beseech thee, O holy and everlasting Father, to forgive these our grievous sins and transgressions, which have provoked thy most just wrath and indignation against us. We beseech thee to remove from our eyes the vail of ignorance, and that we may see light in thy light. Thou hast sent upon us the scourge of war, and we have suffered the spoiling of our goods; our land is overrun and devoured; it is so desolate that all who pass by her do mock at her. Thy churches have been forsaken, destroyed, and desecrated. The remembrance of these our sins and transgressions is most grievous unto us, and we do repent, and are most heartily sorry for the same. And we do beseech thee, O mighty God, holy and everlasting Father, to mitigate the stroke of thy righteous indignation wherewith thou hast stricken us as a people who stand condemned and guilty in thy sight. Grant that all thy penitent people may this day believe in thy most dearly beloved Son, Jesus Christ our Saviour, that through his most precious blood they may find forgiveness of sins, and be cleansed from all unrighteousness. Then, O Father, may the river that maketh glad the city of our God flow through our sanctuaries again; may its life-giving streams flow freely through all our hearts and to all our suffering countrymen, cleansing and purifying the hearts of all. May thy priests be clothed with the robes of holiness; may Zion awake to put on her beautiful garments, and arise from the dust because her Light is come and the glory of the Lord is risen upon her. Grant this, we beseech thee, O most merciful Father, for the sake of our Lord and Saviour Jesus Christ. And to thy name, Father, Son, and Holy Ghost, be all the praise for ever and ever. Amen.